Kid in a Wheelchair: Teaching Children about Others with Disabilities
By Dorothy Scarfone and Michael R Basso

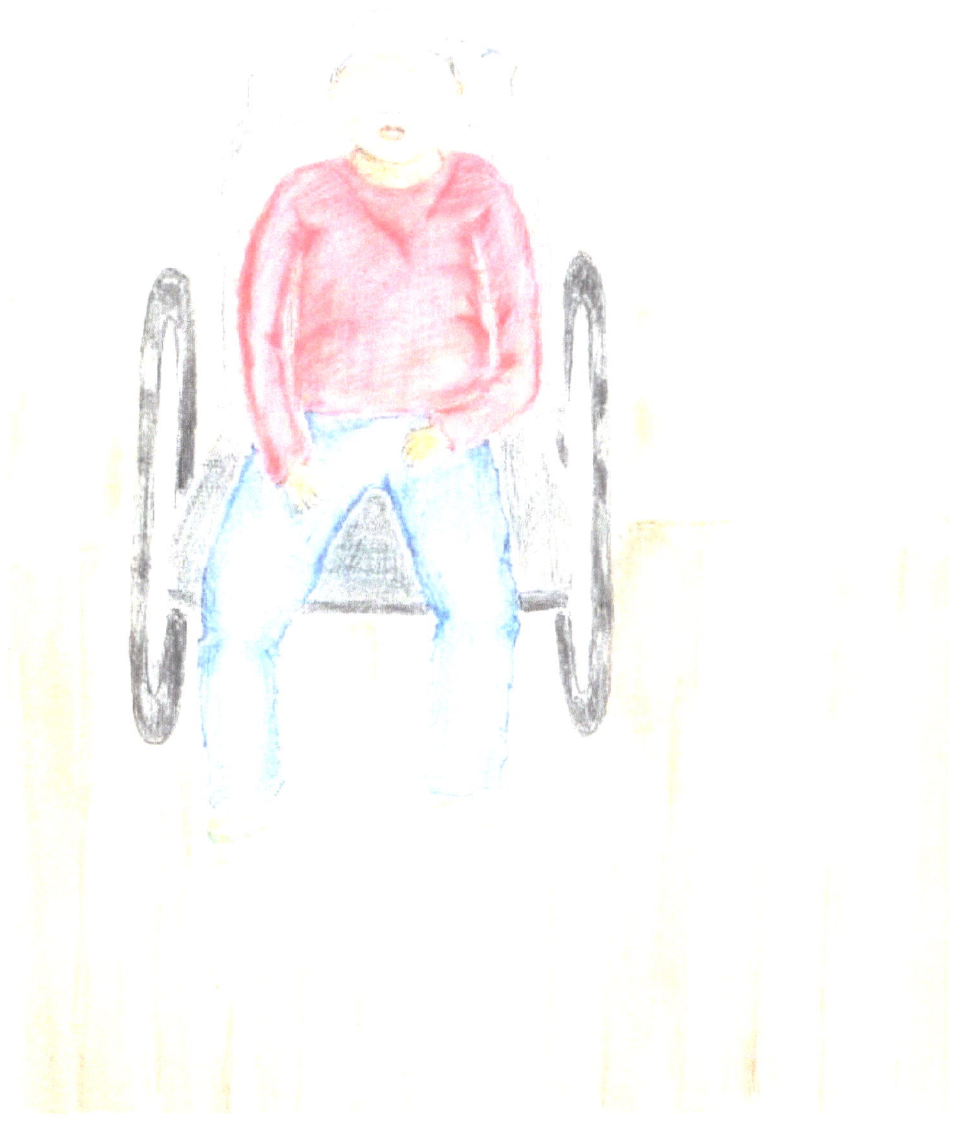

Illustrated By Maria Minnerly-Figueroa

About the Authors

Michael R. Basso has significant experience as a leader in quality and reliability engineering and management in industry, as well as being a college level educator in psychology at Yale University and the University of Connecticut. His experience also includes being a consultant, researcher, and newspaper columnist. Michael is the president of the Connecticut Holistic Health Association.

Dr. Basso has a Ph.D. in professional psychology and biomedical systems, an MS in engineering science, and an MBA with a focus in executive leadership and an interdisciplinary Professional Development Diploma in pathophysiology, neural systems, and education. He also holds a BS in electrical engineering. Michael is certified in quality and reliability engineering and quality auditing, as well as variety of health related areas.

Dorothy lives in New York with Frankie who has Down Syndrome. She has a daughter, Sandra, another son, Mark, and four grandchildren. Dorothy earned an Associates Degree at the Latin-American Institute in Manhattan and her paralegal certificate at Manhattanville College. She now works as a legal secretary/paralegal for a law firm in Greenwich, CT.

Dorothy was a literacy volunteer for many years starting when her children were in elementary school. She has continued to volunteer to teach English to the new wave of immigrants in her native village, Port Chester, NY. She also has been a member of the parish counsel of her church helping to establish goals for the parish. Presently, she is on a committee at her church which reaches out to the elderly. She was also a member of the Board of Directors of Don Bosco Community Center in Port Chester, NY.

Dorothy is also on the Board of Directors of the Tamarack Tower Foundation in Port Chester, NY as well as corresponding secretary for the TTF. She is also on the Board of Directors of the South East Consortium for Special Services, Inc., located in Mamaroneck, NY.

Burt was riding the back seat when it happened. Although his mom asked him to wear a seatbelt, he didn't listen. After the accident, Burt didn't move or speak for weeks. They said that he was in a coma. A coma is like being asleep and not waking up for a long time. Some people never wake up from a coma. Burt was lucky – he did wake up.

It was difficult when he first tried to stand and his legs just didn't move. His legs were paralyzed, so he couldn't use crutches. He had to use a wheelchair.

Mom, "How Did Burt get paralyzed?"

"Well, Jeremy," when the car he was in hit that other car, Burt's spine was hurt real bad.'

"What does that have to do with his legs?"

"The legs are controlled by the brain, Jeremy."

4

"Huh?"

"The body has a 'computer' built into it. Much like when you type into a keyboard, the body's computer gets information from the outside world, then it figures stuff about that information. It might figure that it is best to walk or run or swim…So, the brain tells the legs to move."

"The brain tells the legs to walk through the spinal cord. Feel the bones running through the center of your back. The spine has things like the computer cables you have from the computer to its speakers. The cables are call nerves. One set of nerves
takes

information in from the eyes, ears, nose, mouth, hands and feet…

5

Another set of nerves sends messages out to the arms and legs to make them move."

"When those nerves running from the brain to the legs get hurt badly, they sometimes get cut. If they are cut they usually do not heal like other cuts we may get. Since they often do not heal the person with cut nerves in their spine might not be able to get their legs to move."

"Jeremy, the nerves coming from the brain go through holes in those bones called the spine. When they get close to the legs they split into two smaller nerves – one for the left leg and one for the right."

"Wow! That's cool mom."

"Yes it is, Jeremy."

"Since the nerve is big and contains 'cables' going to each leg before they split, if the nerve gets cut before it splits into nerves for both legs, then both legs might get paralyzed."

"If the nerve gets cut after it splits, then the leg on the side where it gets cut may not be able to move."

"Jeremy, I am going to use some big words that you don't have to remember.

Note*: Kids skip this section if they want to or let their parents or older brothers or sisters read these big words.*

"When both legs don't move the person is sometimes called –

para - pa – legic"

6

"Mom, Marshall's mom's brother couldn't walk and he never got into a car accident. I don't understand why he was paralyzed."

"Well, Jeremy, when Marshall's Uncle Jim was born, he had a problem that caused his brain to get hurt. It was the part of the brain that sent messages to his legs."

"Jeremy, his uncle has what is called –

cer – e – bral palsey"

"It is called that because the top part of the brain is called the cerebrum and 'palsey' means that it stopped working."

"Are there any other ways that someone can get paralyzed?"

"Yes, Jeremy there are. Someone could be born with a *genetic defect* that causes their muscles to not work right. There are several of these diseases, including:

Muscular Dys-tro-phy

and

Mya-sten-ia Grav-is

"You don't have to remember these hard names. But I am telling you them so that you can try to understand better."

"What are genetic defects?"

"Genes are like tiny computers that are inside of us. They tell our bodies how to grow, how tall, what color hair and eyes, the shape of our ears…Sometimes they don't work right, like when we have to call the computer guy to help us fix our computer. With people it is sometimes not that easy."

"There are also genetic diseases that don't let the covering over the nerves to work. Two of these diseases are called

Mul-tiple Scler-o-sis (MS)

A-L-S"

"When the covering over the nerves gets messed up it's like a computer cable with no covering. Sometimes one nerve messes up other nerve – then sometimes the person can walk and at other times they can not. Weather and even certain foods can make these people walk or not walk…. Some people with MS cannot walk when the weather gets cold. Some people with those diseases are helped by nutrients in their foods like 'sunflower oil' or even oil from plants – like 'evening primrose oil.'"

"People can also get infections that damage the nerves – like

Po-li-o."

"Jeremy, please hold the door open for Mrs. Smith. She's pushing Burt into school for the first time in a wheelchair."

"OK, mom."

"Oh Mommy, I am soooooo embarrassed!!!!!!!," Burt cried out to his mom as she pushed him into the classroom."

Sally cried when she saw Burt in a wheelchair.

This made Burt even more embarrassed.

"Poor Burt," Jeremy thought as he saw his good friend being pushed into the classroom.

The first day was OK, until the end of the day.

Ted, Burt's best friend somehow forgot and asked Burt if he was going to play baseball after…..school.

"Oh, I am so sorry, Burt…I forgot……"

Burt cried and cried and cried – that whole night. When he went to bed all he could do was to think about what it was like to watch his friends playing his favorite sport – baseball – in the park right outside of his living room window.

Mrs. Sparrow, I have to go to bathroom," Burt called out in class the next day.

"I'll have to call the nurse to help you."

"Noooooo. Please not that!!!!!"

"OK, Burt, we'll call your dad today, since he is home today and real close by. But he has to get you a male aide to help you if that's what you want."

Burt was soooo embarrassed and sad….he began to cry and cry. Mrs. Sparrow sent him home for the rest of the day – for his sake, but also because he was disrupting the other kids and making them sad because they felt sorry for him.

When Burt and Jeremy returned to school the next day, Mrs. Sparrow had a vacant wheelchair in the front of the classroom. The children looked around and wondered aloud what this was all about. Mrs. Sparrow said, "Class, today we're going to have an experiment. One by one, we are each going to spend one day in this Wheelchair in order to learn what Burt is

experiencing." The one rule that Mrs. Sparrow had was that under no circumstances were you to get out of the chair.

Jeremy was the first to volunteer for the experiment. "This will be a piece of cake," said Jeremy. I won't have to walk all day.

Mrs. Sparrow began the class assignment by handing out test questions. When Jeremy got his paper, he dropped it and started to get out of the wheelchair in order to pick up the test paper. Mrs. Sparrow simply shook her head and asked if he would like someone to pick up the paper for him. Jeremy complied. He then realized that he would be needing help all day long.

After taking the test, Jeremy raised his hand for permission to go to the boy's room. Mrs. Sparrow said yes. When Jeremy wheeled himself through the door of the classroom, his fingers got stuck in the doorway and were bruised. He rubbed his fingers and thought what a bother this wheelchair was becoming.

When Jeremy arrived at the boy's room, he discovered that the doorknob was hard to reach. He had to maneuver the wheelchair so he was sideways in front of the door instead of directly in front of it. He finally, after several tries, was able to turn the doorknob and enter the boy's room. Here Jeremy soon discovered more problems which, with the help of another boy, he was able to overcome.

"This is not going to be easy," thought Jeremy. "Poor Burt will have to deal with this forever."

"Poor Burt," Jeremy thought to himself, when he has to pee, or worse, O God!, somebody has to help him. Who is going to wipe his butt ??? Yuk. What about taking a shower?"

At recess, Jeremy wanted to play baseball with the other boys but this was impossible. However, he was able to play a sort of dodge ball with the girls. Jeremy was not happy about this.

When Jeremy got home with his wheelchair his mother rushed outside wondering what had happened. He explained to her about the experiment.

Jeremy had his afternoon snack, did his homework and played computer games all from his chair.

It was time to take a shower and then get into his PJ's. Now what? He forgot if Mrs. Sparrow really wanted him to do all that stuff or just pretend.

Jeremy thought it was Reeeeeeal lucky for him that no one was really going to help him get undressed or take a shower or wipe his butt……but poor Burt, he thought, oh poor Burt…..

Sally reported to the class about her experiences over the weekend.

Her parents were acting real weird when they wheeled her into the expensive country club dining room where they ate Saturday night. Her dad acted like he was ashamed to be around her. He avoided his daughter the whole night, while he talked to his 'high class' friends.

"They didn't seem that high class to me, Mrs Sparrow. Who cares how much money they have? I don't – neither does my mom. The acted like A…"

15

"Ok I get the point, Sally, please don't swear. I know this experience upset you. It seemed that you really learned some important lessons."

"Yes I did, Mrs. Sparrow."

"Some of my dad's friends are jerks"

"Stop that, Sally."

"OK."

"Billy, what happened to you?"

"My brother took me to the beach. It was great. All the 'babes' ignored him and they felt sorry for me. How funny!!! _ I'm the one they usually ignore."

The class was in an uproar.

"Burt had a smile on his face. Wow - maybe I can make the most out of this situation – even though I don't want people to be my friend just because I am 'sick.'"

Mrs. Sparrow knew that Burt needed ways to build his self-esteem more than anything else. She knew that Burt was real good at math…

"OK everyone – we haven't had a 'math B' for awhile…."

Burt won like he always did. But this time he appreciated his success more than he ever did. It was clear from the expression that he was real happy and real sad at the same time.

"Katie, what happened to you?"

"Well, one of my mom's friends thought I should learn to meditate. She asked me to keep my feet on the floor – how funny!"

"Go on, Katie."

"It did make me feel good. She asked me to take a few deep breaths and then to pick a word that I liked, Hu, OM, one…. And say that word that I choose to myself for about 10 minutes."

"I tried it both Saturday and Sunday and while it seemed weird, I did feel more relaxed."

Susan replied, "My mom's friend asked her to tell me to tell Burt's mom to make sure that he has a lot of B-Vitamins, whatever they are, in his

food, along with Zinc, Magnesium, Omega 3….and a few other things. She also said that it would be great to get Burt some puzzles to help relax him and keep his mind occupied."

Mrs. Sparrow told a story about how her friend Dot's dad was in a wheelchair for many years. "He learned to start his own home business – he did taxes, made copies of things and did lots to bring in some extra income. He also was able to swim several times a week to keep his body strong. When he was in the water he could float and it was easy for him to at least do a few things that way. Sometimes when someone looses the use of either their arms or legs, they use the other limbs to help them move in the water – even if they are slow…."

"Then someone has to change them at the pool," Melvin asked.

"Usually some arrangement has to be made, Melvin…but they can sometimes get changed at home if that works better."

"OooooK, Mrs. Sparrow. Thank God nobody has to change me like a baby….Yuk and double Yuk……"

19

Copyright © 2011 By Michael R Basso and Dorothy Scarfone

"Ok, Melvin we get the point."

Even Burt laughed, but everyone knew that he was also crying inside.

"My sister is a nurse," Jenny said – "and she told me about this guy, Norman Cousins, who was very sick and used funny movies and laughter to help when he was sick – he lived MANY years beyond how long they said he would. She pretended that I was really sick and made me watch some really funny movies. It did make me feel good even though I could go dancing with my friends. I guess I could have, but…."

Don chimed in and let the class know that his dad is an interfaith minister and that he told Don that "….a strong belief in God or something spiritual can help sick people to gain a sense of hope about getting better. Sometimes when they think that they are going to die soon – like Don's grandfather, spirituality or religion can help them to feel more confident about what happens after they die."

"Very good, class. I see that you all learned something useful. That's all for today."

Workbook Section

Note that it is OK to ask for help with this section.

Please name three ways that people can get paralyzed:

1)

2)

3)

What are the 'cables' called that send messages from your brain to your legs (or arms) to make them move?

Please Answer Here:

Please name five challenges that people in wheelchairs and their families must overcome and how they would affect you.

1)

2)

3)

4)

5)

Please define self-esteem and write down three ways that someone can help someone with a disability to improve their self-esteem.

Definition:

Ways to improve self-esteem (Please be creative).

1)

2)

3)

What are some nutritional things that have helped children with disabilities to relax and maybe do other things to help them get stronger?

1)

2)

3)

4)

5)

Please name five other things that may help people in wheel chairs.

1)

2)

3)

4)

5)

In this section, please give us some examples of how religion or spirituality can help someone with a disability or their families. Thank You.

1)

2)

3)

4)

5)

6)

What would it be like if you were in a wheelchair?

1)

2)

3)

4)

5)

29

If you could invent a better wheelchair or something better than a wheelchair, what would you invention be like?

What kind of games would you play with a child who is in a wheelchair?

1)

2)

3)

4)

5)

6)

7)

Notes: